Economically Developing Countries

Nigeria

Alasdair Tenquist

Wayland

Economically Developing Countries

Bangladesh	**Mexico**
Brazil	**Korea**
China	**Malaysia**
Egypt	**Nigeria**
Ghana	**Peru**
India	**Vietnam**

Cover: Fulani women from northern Nigeria carry firewood and water in pots on their heads.
Title page: Buying fish from the boats on the banks of the River Niger.
Contents page: The Argungu fishing festival in north-west Nigeria.

Picture acknowledgements:
Camera Press 42; J. Allan Cash Photo Library 33; Robert Estall Photos 15 (top); Mary Evans Picture Library 12 (bottom); Eye Ubiquitous 17, 22, 35; Impact Photos *Cover*, 3, 4 (main), 14, 26, 27, 28, 29, 37 (top & bottom); Robert Harding Picture Library 5, 8, 18, 19, 24, 25, 32, 43, 44; James H. Morris *Title page*, 4 (inset), 34; Panos Pictures 6, 7 (top & bottom), 9, 10, 15 (bottom), 16, 20, 21, 23, 25, 38, 39, 40, 41, 45 (top & bottom); Popperfoto 13, 30, 31 (top & bottom); Werner Forman Archive 11, 12 (top).

Series editor: Paul Mason
Book editor: Polly Goodman
Designer: Mark Whitchurch
Picture researcher: Shelley Noronha

First published in 1996 by
Wayland (Publishers) Ltd
61 Western Road, Hove
East Sussex, BN3 1JD, England

British Library Cataloguing in Publication Data
Tenquist, Alasdair
    Nigeria. - (Economically Developing
    Countries Series)
    I. Title II. Series
    966.9053

ISBN 0 7502 1572 0

Typeset by Mark Whitchurch, England
Printed and bound in Italy by G. Canale & C.S.p.A., Turin

Contents

Introduction

The Federal Republic of Nigeria, or 'giant of Africa', is a large country in West Africa named after the River Niger. It has the highest population in Africa, and is home to one in five of all Africans.

Nigeria has a proud history of great civilizations, kingdoms and empires. But the country we know as Nigeria was only formed in 1960, and half its population is less than fifteen years old. Over the last thirty-five years Nigeria's government has been very unstable, with changing leaders and styles of government causing frequent military coups and violence.

An incredible mix of cultures lives in Nigeria, with over 250 different tribes. Each tribe has its own language, traditions and religion, and each struggles for the right to decide its own future. The intense rivalry between these tribes affects the politics of the country as a whole.

There is a striking contrast in standards of living. Nigeria is one of the world's major producers of oil, and the vast wealth that has come from this industry has helped to make some Nigerians very rich, and to build huge, modern cities. Yet it seems that the vast majority of the population has been untouched by this wealth. Many city dwellers are crowded into run-down flats with no water or electricity, and two-thirds of the population live a difficult existence on tiny farms, using agricultural methods unchanged for centuries.

A Hausa chief's guard in north-west Nigeria.

THE NIGERIAN FLAG

The green of the flag represents agriculture and fertility. The white represents unity and peace.

A villager and his children in the traditional village of Zaraguta, near Jos in central Nigeria.

NIGERIA AT A GLANCE	
Population:	101 million (1995 estimate)
Capital:	Abuja (population 300,000)
Area:	923,768 km²
Currency:	Naira (N)
Language:	Officially English. Most Nigerians also speak Yoruba, Hausa or Ibo.
Religion:	North: Islam South: Christianity Many Nigerians still practise traditional African religions.
Foundation:	1 October 1960
Head of State:	General Sani Abacha

Nigeria is a fascinating country, with proud, hospitable and good-humoured peoples. It is also a 'sleeping giant', rich in natural resources, many of which are as yet untapped. As many of its people often say, it is 'an economic miracle waiting to happen.' However, Nigeria has many problems. Apart from its political unrest, it has a rapidly increasing population and decreasing national income. Increasingly, poorer families have more mouths to feed, while the government finds it more and more difficult to provide for basic needs such as jobs, health care and education. The result is poverty, homelessness and increasingly violent protests.

5

Land and climate

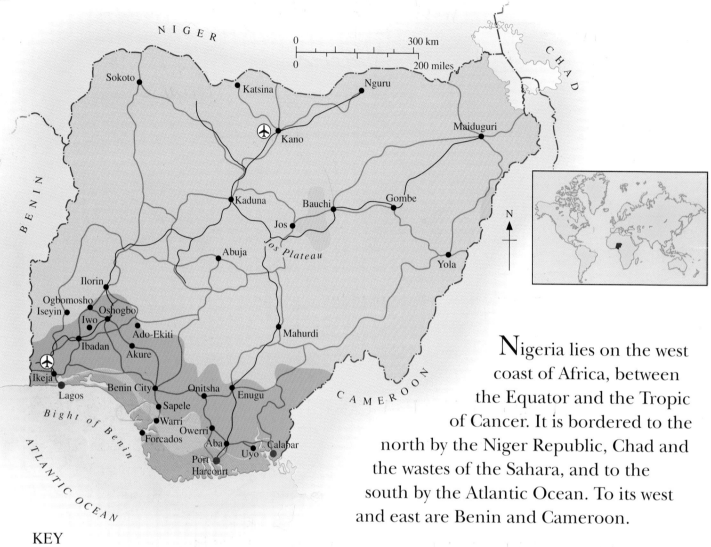

KEY

— Major roads
— Railways
● Major ports
✈ International airports

VEGETATION ZONES
- Savannah
- Rainforest
- Freshwater swamp forest
- Mangrove swamp forest
- Plateau grasslands

Nigeria lies on the west coast of Africa, between the Equator and the Tropic of Cancer. It is bordered to the north by the Niger Republic, Chad and the wastes of the Sahara, and to the south by the Atlantic Ocean. To its west and east are Benin and Cameroon.

VEGETATION

There is an incredible variety of landscapes in Nigeria. In the far south are lagoons, mangrove swamps and innumerable streams around the Gulf of Guinea and the Bight of Benin. Before malaria tablets and modern health care, this hot, humid area was notoriously hostile to foreigners, with disease and death common.

Inland, the landscape changes to dense tropical rainforest. Over 3,000 mm of rain falls here each year, although it is heaviest in the wet season, from March to October. The constant high temperatures (between 25–28 °C) and rainfall mean that there is a luxuriant growth of vegetation, with a stunning variety of plants and animals.

6

Further north the rainforest gradually clears, to more open woodland and the grassy plains and isolated trees of the drier savannah region. Here the days are hot and the nights cool. There is normally a rainy season – a belt of rain usually sweeps north each year from the southern rainforests, to reach the central and northern regions around July. All too often, however, the rains stop short. Farmers in the savannah are used to drought and dried-up river beds, and they have dug deep wells to reach the scarce and precious water supplies.

A deep water-hole is the only source of water in this drought-hit area near Jos.

MANGROVE SWAMPS

Nigeria's coast has many miles of sandy beaches and lagoons, but just behind these lie mangrove swamps. These are forests of mangrove trees which have tall 'stilt' roots. The roots keep the main part of the tree out of the tidal waters. They also help to trap silt and goodness from the water and provide protection for many types of fish and animals.

The climate of the mangrove swamps is hot, wet and humid, very similar to the rainforest climate. It has always been an unpopular climate with travellers. One early explorer wrote of 'an indescribable feeling of heaviness ... which requires a considerable effort to shake off.' The constant threat of malaria also makes the area a difficult place to live. There is very little dry land, so the population is thinly spread. The local people survive by fishing along a maze of tiny channels which wind between the trees.

The stilt roots of a mangrove tree, holding it above the water at high tide.

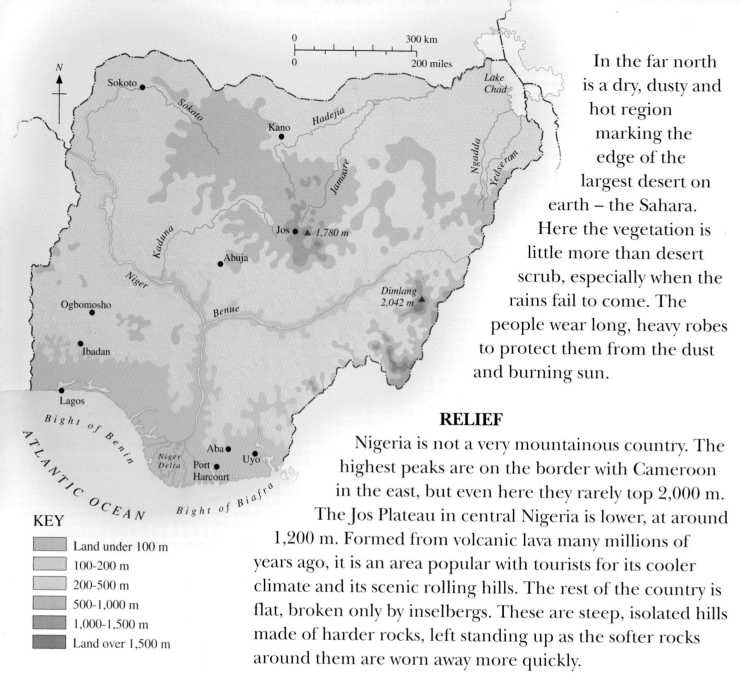

In the far north is a dry, dusty and hot region marking the edge of the largest desert on earth – the Sahara. Here the vegetation is little more than desert scrub, especially when the rains fail to come. The people wear long, heavy robes to protect them from the dust and burning sun.

KEY

Land under 100 m
100-200 m
200-500 m
500-1,000 m
1,000-1,500 m
Land over 1,500 m

RELIEF

Nigeria is not a very mountainous country. The highest peaks are on the border with Cameroon in the east, but even here they rarely top 2,000 m. The Jos Plateau in central Nigeria is lower, at around 1,200 m. Formed from volcanic lava many millions of years ago, it is an area popular with tourists for its cooler climate and its scenic rolling hills. The rest of the country is flat, broken only by inselbergs. These are steep, isolated hills made of harder rocks, left standing up as the softer rocks around them are worn away more quickly.

Shepherds stand on the Panyam volcano, in Plateau state, Central Nigeria.

'*I catch fish from the River Niger. At the end of each day I mend any broken nets. I sell some of the fish in the local market at Onitsha. The rest I dry and salt in the sun, and sell it for a good price in Lagos.*'
– **Anthony Alfa, fisherman from the Rivers State, in the Niger Delta.**

Fishing on the River Niger at Onitsha. Thousands of fishing families rely on the river for their livelihood.

RIVERS AND DAMS

The great River Niger, after which Nigeria is named, rises in Guinea and flows through Mali and Niger before entering north-west Nigeria. It then flows south-east until it joins up with the River Benue, from where it winds south to the Gulf of Guinea. Much of the river's course is unnavigable, due to rapids in the high season, or low flow in the dry season. As it reaches the ocean, the Niger slows down, splits into several channels and deposits millions of tonnes of mud and silt. This fans out into the Gulf of Guinea, forming a huge delta some 320 km wide.

THE ANNUAL 'BLACK FLOOD'

The 'Black Flood' affects large areas of the Niger river valley as it winds its way through the flat plains of north-west Nigeria. Each year the river's level is raised several metres, covering the floodplain on either side. While this can damage crops and buildings, it also brings life-giving water and nutrient-rich mud for the thirsty crops growing there.

The origin of the flood can be found over 6,000 km away in Guinea, at the source of the River Niger. Here there is a marked wet season around August and September. The water rushes into the Niger, and the swollen waters glide down the river at the rate of 17 km per day, taking six months to reach Nigeria.

The floods in the southern part of the country are now controlled by a series of dams along the river's course. The biggest of these is Kainji Dam, 400 m wide and 70 m high.

The River Niger is dammed in several places, forming huge lakes. The largest of these is the Kainji Reservoir in the north-west of the country, which is over 180 km long (see page 33). Apart from providing irrigation for the dry savannah plains, the dams are also a useful source of electricity for the surrounding region.

WILDLIFE

Nigeria's wildlife is abundant. The wide open grasslands and occasional woodland of the savannah are ideal for grazing animals such as antelopes and gazelle. These are preyed upon by lions and leopards. Herds of elephants, baboons and buffalo also roam the plains, while around the rivers there are hippopotamuses, crocodiles and fish eagles. In the southern forests live monkeys, chimpanzees and giant forest hogs. The wildlife is being threatened by human overpopulation, however, and the rapid destruction of Nigeria's forests. Many of the animals are now confined to a few national game reserves, such as the Yankari Reserve, east of the Jos Plateau. The number of animal species threatened with extinction in Nigeria is the second highest in the world.

Elephants in the Yankari Game Reserve, Bauchi State.

The peoples of Nigeria

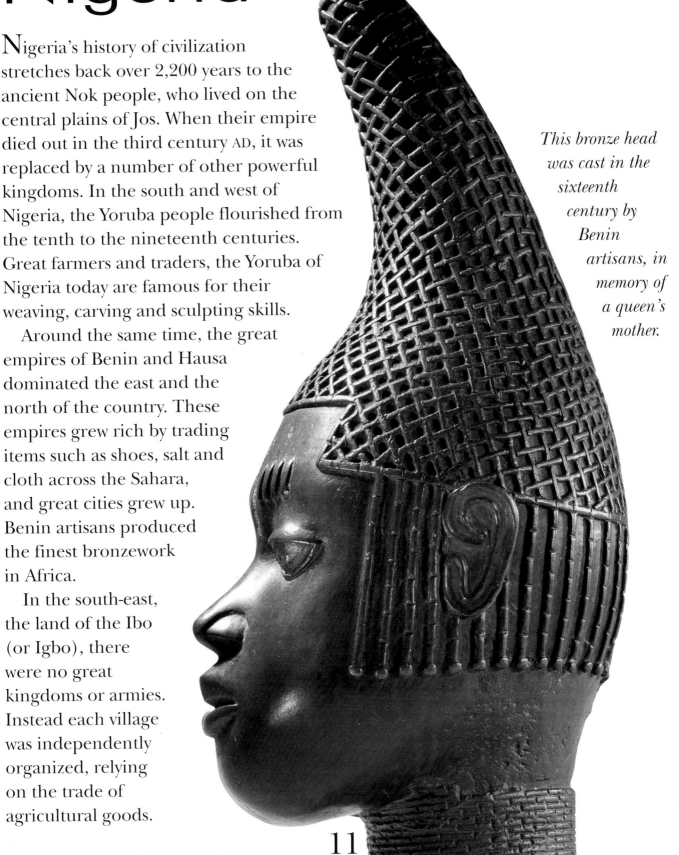

Nigeria's history of civilization stretches back over 2,200 years to the ancient Nok people, who lived on the central plains of Jos. When their empire died out in the third century AD, it was replaced by a number of other powerful kingdoms. In the south and west of Nigeria, the Yoruba people flourished from the tenth to the nineteenth centuries. Great farmers and traders, the Yoruba of Nigeria today are famous for their weaving, carving and sculpting skills.

Around the same time, the great empires of Benin and Hausa dominated the east and the north of the country. These empires grew rich by trading items such as shoes, salt and cloth across the Sahara, and great cities grew up. Benin artisans produced the finest bronzework in Africa.

In the south-east, the land of the Ibo (or Igbo), there were no great kingdoms or armies. Instead each village was independently organized, relying on the trade of agricultural goods.

This bronze head was cast in the sixteenth century by Benin artisans, in memory of a queen's mother.

A carving showing a Yoruba king (left) receiving the first British administrator (right) in about 1900.

In 1472, the Portuguese arrived in Nigeria and began trading for gold, spices and ivory. Soon they and other European countries turned to the slave trade, in which individual Nigerian kingdoms readily exchanged captured prisoners for guns and cloth. In the 350 years that followed, an estimated 2 million Nigerians were forcefully shipped to the Americas to work on plantations in European colonies there. The Nigerian empires grew weaker as they fought each other for control of this cruel trade with Europe.

SLAVE TRADE

The slave trade ran from the beginning of the sixteenth century until its abolition in 1807. European countries including Britain, Spain and Portugal needed workers for their plantations in the Caribbean and South America. So they shipped out black slaves from Nigeria.

Most slaves were captives taken in wars between Nigerian tribes. Others were convicted murderers or thieves, while some were unlucky enough to be abducted by gangs of slave hunters. The traders then brought their victims to the coastal markets in chains.

The slaves were sold and ushered on to boats waiting for the Atlantic journey to the Americas. The horror of the Atlantic passage is difficult to imagine, and diseases such as measles, scurvy and smallpox, were common. In 1726, two ships, the Sea Horse and the St Michael, lost more than 600 of the 1,030 slaves they carried to disease.

'Their way of bringing them is tying them by the neck with leather thongs, at about a yard distant from each other, thirty or forty in a string, having generally a bundle of corn, or an elephant's tooth upon each of their heads.'
— **European slave buyer in Nigeria, sixteenth century.**

Slaves are taken down to the coast to an awaiting ship. Below them is a plan showing how the slaves were packed into the ships.

In the Berlin Conference of 1883, Africa was divided up and distributed amongst the European powers and Nigeria became a British colony. Many plantations were developed, exporting groundnuts, cocoa and other goods to Britain, until Nigeria finally became an independent nation in 1960.

Since independence, however, right up until today, Nigeria has had a violent history, marked by coups and civil unrest. For twenty-four of its thirty-five years since independence, Nigeria has been under military rule. In June 1992, President Babangida promised democratic elections, but immediately cancelled the results because he claimed the voting had not been fair. He also imprisoned the winner of the cancelled presidential elections.

THE BIAFRAN WAR

One of the worst chapters in Nigeria's violent history was the Biafran war between 1967–70.

In 1967, the Ibo declared an independent Republic of Biafra in the south-east of the country, and civil war broke out. France entered the war by supporting the Ibo, since it hoped to gain oil-drilling rights in the area. South Africa, Côte D'Ivoire, Portugal and Rhodesia also supported the Ibo, because they wanted to see the Nigerian government's power in the region reduced. The USA backed the Nigerian government, but most of the world's press were in sympathy with the Ibo, who were being starved into surrender by government forces. Eventually, after three harrowing years of disease, malnutrition and fighting, in which over a million people died, Nigerian troops overran the area and the Republic of Biafra ceased to exist.

Truckloads of Ibo refugees from the civil war flock into the city of Owerri in 1970.

13

A Fulani girl from northern Nigeria.

Nigeria's population tod⋯ stands at about 100 million. However, it is increasing rapidly, doubling every nineteen years. The main source of the population increase is the countryside, where in many areas it is traditional for families to have a minimum of at least ten children to help on the farms.

There are over 250 different tribes in Nigeria. The four most powerful are the Hausa and Fulani in the north, the Ibo in the south-east, and the Yoruba in the west around Lagos and Ibadan. Together these make up two-thirds of Nigeria's total population. But there is great rivalry between all the tribes, with each demanding to have its share of the power and government funding that is given to regional areas. It is because of this rivalry that the number of states has grown from three in 1960 to thirty-one in 1995, each state being governed by a particular tribe.

CENSUS CHEATING

Nigeria has boasted for years of having the largest population in Africa. However, in 1991 it had to reduce its own population estimate from over 120 million down to just 88.5 million. This followed a United Nations census of the same year which discovered cheating in the registering process. Over 20 million 'ghost' voters were removed from the census register, names that had been illegally added to the voting list in previous years.

The reason for this 'cheating' was the regional rivalries between the Hausa/Fulani-dominated north and the Yoruba/Ibo-dominated south. The more people an area has, the more money it is given by the government. Therefore regional leaders gave wildly exaggerated head counts to gain a bigger slice of the national 'cake'.

'People were begging to be counted because they know that when the planning of resources begins, they will be left out if their community is not registered.'
– Okereka Kingsley, a census worker in Port Harcourt.

Festivals hold a vital place in Nigerian society. Every important occasion – the birth of a child, a child's 'coming of age', the beginning and end of the harvest, and many others – are marked by celebrations, dance and music.

Each religion has its own calendar of festivals, many of which can last for days. This means that there is rarely a day without a festival going on somewhere close. It also means that there is a stunning variety of celebrations. In the north, for example, the end of Ramadan, the Muslim month of fasting, is marked by a *sallah*. In this festival, everybody in the cities and surrounding villages dresses in their most colourful clothes and hats. Carrying bright flags and umbrellas, they make their way in a spectacular parade from the city prayer ground to the square in front of the emir's (governor's) palace, with the emir and his troops bringing up the rear. Horsemen from each of the surrounding villages take it in turns to charge up to the emir, stopping within inches of his throne to salute him with a raised right fist. Last, and most fierce, are the emir's bodyguards. The emir then addresses the crowds to cheers and applause. The noise, splendour and colour are unforgettable.

One of the more interesting festivals is held by the Woodaabe people of eastern Nigeria. Here the village warriors compete for the title of 'most beautiful and charming man'. The judges are women. The men wear colourful make-up emphasizing their eyes and teeth.

Above *Woodaabe dancers in their festival costumes and make-up.*

Left *An emir and his guards on* sallah *day.*

Religion is also divided according to the tribes. In the north, the Hausa-Fulani are Muslim and practise Islam. In many northern areas there are calls to return to strict Islamic rules such as 'purdah' for women. This demands that women wear headscarves, veils and long gowns to cover their heads, arms and legs from the sight of men. It is common to hear the 'call to prayer' in these Muslim areas, a daily event where many people stop what they are doing and kneel on special carpets, chanting their prayers. The south of the country is dominated by Christianity, with the Protestant Yoruba in the south-west, and the Catholic Ibo in the south-east.

Some Nigerians still practise animism, especially in the more isolated rural areas. This is the belief that natural objects, such as trees and stones, have their own spirits. Animists also worship their ancestors, whose spirits, they believe, protect the earth and its people.

Language is another source of division. Although English is the official language, there are over 400 languages and dialects used in Nigeria. The main spoken language in the north is Hausa, in the east it is Ibo, and in the west it is Yoruba. There have been attempts to combine these languages into one, but they have all failed.

Language is often used to maintain and develop tribal traditions. Stories, legends, poems and songs are recited over and over again to pass on the history, culture and religion of the tribe to succeeding generations.

A Muslim man at prayer in Kaduna, central Nigeria.

The Fulani

The Fulani people live in northern Nigeria, where they are famous as herders of cattle, sheep and goats. They are traditionally a nomadic people, constantly keeping on the move to find fresh pastures for their herds. In this part of Nigeria, the number of cattle a person owns is still a measure of wealth and importance, and many Fulani hold important positions within the region.

'I find the wet season very hard. We have to keep the cattle moving over waterlogged ground and the camps are muddy and dirty. It is very humid and uncomfortable and the flies get everywhere – in your clothes, in your hair, biting all the time.'
– Chirima Yola, Fulani herdsboy.

A group of Fulani herd their cattle.

There are two types of Fulani in Nigeria today. One type, the *Borroro-je* (or 'cow Fulani'), have a wandering lifestyle, following the rains with their cattle. They have an expert knowledge of the landscape, the rainfall pattern and where water is available at different times of the year. As a result, the *Borroro-je* have been able to take advantage of what pasture is available, even in years when rainfall is below average. In the dry season they move south to the River Niger, and in the wet season they move north to the freshly watered plains bordering the Sahara desert. The *Borroro-je* are an independent people who only marry amongst themselves.

The other type, the *Fulani Gidda* (*Gidda* means compound), gave up their wandering lifestyle and settled down in the cities. There they quickly took up important positions. The emirs (governors) of the great northern cities today are descendants of those original *Fulani Gidda*.

Many nomadic Fulani are now exchanging their old way of life in favour of the city. Others are semi-nomadic, which means they have a small farm as well as cattle to herd.

In the city

Even though most Nigerians live in the countryside, Nigeria has some of the largest and fastest-growing cities in Africa. The biggest of these is Lagos, Nigeria's main city and ex-capital.

There has been a settlement on Lagos Island, the heart of the modern city, since the Portuguese established a port there in the fifteenth century to trade with the kingdom of Benin (Lagos means 'lagoon' in Portuguese). Lagos soon became a wealthy city as trade in gold and other items gave way to the slave trade. In 1861, Britain took control of Lagos and from there its rule spread over the whole of what is now Nigeria.

By 1950, Lagos Island had become an overcrowded slum area. So the decision was taken to evict the 200,000 or so people living there and turn the whole area into a modern central city area. Gleaming tower blocks and modern shops and offices replaced what had been shacks and run-down dwellings.

Tinubu Square in Lagos, Nigeria's former capital city.

In the last thirty years, the city has grown many times, to its present population of about 1.4 million people. It is the fastest-growing major city in the world, mostly due to poor migrants from the countryside flooding into the city in search of a new life. In 1950, less than one in every hundred Nigerians lived in Lagos. Now the figure is one in fifteen, and rapidly increasing. The city cannot cope with this population explosion, and huge, unplanned poor areas have been the result. These are not like the makeshift shanty towns found in many developing world cities. They are generally solidly built, permanent dwellings, called 'popular settlements'.

One such area is Olaleye village. At one time the village was a farming community, but it has long been swallowed up by the growth of Lagos. Few houses have electricity or water supplies. Open sewers carry the constant threat of disease, and food, fuel and building materials are in short supply. The area is not serviced in the same way as other parts of the city, and rubbish piles up in unofficial dumps. Olaleye, like other popular settlements, is built on one of the least attractive parts of the city. Its low-lying site means that its inhabitants have to cope with the constant threat of flooding.

POPULATION GROWTH, LAGOS STATE.

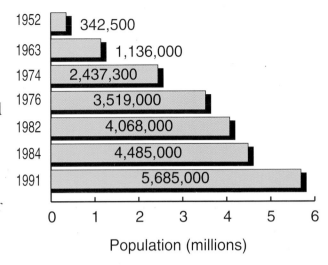

Year	Population
1952	342,500
1963	1,136,000
1974	2,437,300
1976	3,519,000
1982	4,068,000
1984	4,485,000
1991	5,685,000

Population (millions)

'It can be hard living here. My father is a taxi driver but there's not much work around for him. My mother works as a maid for one of the rich families in the centre of the city but there is never enough money for our food, clothes, rent and fuel for the taxi.' – *Chidi Adibeyo, 13 years old, resident of Olaleye popular settlement.*

A popular settlement on Lagos Island.

19

Lagos has a number of big modern factories, which use the latest technology to produce high quality goods. However, most people work in the informal (illegal) sector, working long hours for low pay in back-street shacks. Many others sell goods for little money on the city streets, shouting out their wares as they pass from car to car in the city's notorious traffic jams.

There has been much city growth in other areas of Nigeria too. The new capital city of Abuja has been built over the past fifteen years in the central plains of Nigeria. It now covers 250 km² and has a population of 300,000. Abuja was built to decrease the growing pressure on Lagos and, despite some setbacks, it seems to have had some success. Embassies, industries and many branches of the government have moved there to enjoy ithe city's modern facilities. It increasingly seems that Abuja will be the place that foreign dignitaries and businesspeople have to visit if they wish to see Nigerian government officials.

TRAFFIC 'GO SLOWS'

Lagos is notorious for its 'go slows', or long traffic jams. Despite a new network of motorways and flyovers, whole districts, including the city centre, are often paralysed for much of the day.

The frustration caused by the jams often spills over into quarrels and even bloodshed on the city streets. However, the motorists stuck in their cars provide an ideal market for teams of hawkers selling anything from newspapers to televisions and video recorders.

Opposite *The national mosque in the new capital city of Abuja.*

Left *Vendors in Lagos selling their goods on the city streets. Drivers caught in the 'go slows' of Lagos provide a ready market for street sellers like these.*

The ancient part of Kano city, with its houses made of dried mud.

Another important city in northern Nigeria is the ancient walled city of the Hausa kingdom, Kano. Founded many centuries ago, Kano has now grown well beyond its old walls. However the medieval central area still has its original low flat roofs, open courtyards and thick, sun-baked mud walls. These have kept the people inside cool in the day and warm at night for centuries.

Crime in Lagos

One of the side effects of the growing poverty in Lagos has been a crime wave sweeping through the city. Gangs of robbers roam the wealthy districts at night, preying on the people who live behind barbed wire fences and security guards. These have been joined by the 'area boys', gangs of youths armed with clubs who terrorize traders, ransack shops and mug motorists.

Another problem is heavily armed gangs of car thieves from the neighbouring country of Benin, who enter Nigeria under cover of darkness, escaping in convoys of the latest car models. Shoot-outs on the city roads are common.

Drugs are becoming an increasing source of income for many in Lagos. It is estimated that at least six major drug-trafficking groups operate within Nigeria. A common trick is for heroin from Thailand, and cocaine from Brazil, to be placed in condoms or balloons and consumed with a thick okra soup. The drugs are then retrieved after the carrier has flown to Europe or the USA, and sold for high prices on the city streets.

In the countryside

Despite the rapidly growing cities, over two-thirds of Nigerians still live and work in the countryside. Apart from oil, the countryside is Nigeria's greatest source of wealth.

Most of this wealth is earned from large-scale farms in the south of the country, called plantations. Crops are produced using modern machinery, chemicals and disease-resistant seeds. There are relatively few workers needed, but those that are used are generally highly skilled. There are also large-scale farms in the savannah areas further north, but these generally need major irrigation projects to supplement their limited water supplies. The crops produced on these farms are not food crops, such as maize and cassava, which could be used to feed the hungry millions in Nigeria. Instead they are export crops such as cocoa, groundnuts and palm oil, which are sold abroad in an attempt to pay off the huge debts that Nigeria owes to other countries.

FARMING IN NIGERIA			
	1970	1980	1990
Percentage of population employed in agriculture	71%	68%	65%
Tractors in use	2,900	8,600	11,000
Use of fertilizer (kg per hectare)	0.2	3.4	6.0

Modern machinery like this tractor is used mainly on the large-scale farms. However, most of Nigeria's farmers cannot afford to buy, run or maintain such machinery.

'A new class of farmers is emerging in this country ... businessmen and landowners who now see agriculture as a new frontier for becoming wealthy or for storing their windfall wealth.'
– **from *New Nigerian*, 1982.**

23

AGRICULTURAL PRODUCTION
(thousand tonnes)

- Cassava
- Millet
- Maize
- Plantains
- Groundnuts
- Cocoa beans, rubber and cotton

Source: *FAO Production Yearbook, 1992.*

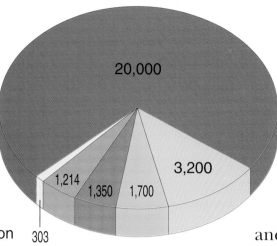

20,000

3,200

1,700

1,350

1,214

303

Women on a subsistence farm pick the wheat crop by hand without the help of expensive machinery.

In stark contrast to the plantations, the majority of people in the countryside live simple lives that have not changed for centuries. They work with simple tools on tiny farms called smallholdings, producing enough food for themselves and their family. This is called subsistence farming. A small surplus is produced which is sold or exchanged for other necessary goods in the local village market. Unlike the large-scale farms, several crops are grown in the same field, but planted at different times. As one crop is harvested, the next crop is given room to spread and ripen, a process known as intercropping. This process has the advantage that the soil is rarely left exposed to erosion. Another common practise is crop rotation, where a field will have different crops grown on it in successive years, including a year of fallow (rest), so that the soil can be kept fertile.

The Nigerian market

Nearly all food and clothes shopping is carried out at Nigeria's famous open-air markets. There is a stunning variety of locally produced goods on display at these events. Many Nigerians prefer these local markets to the modern shops in the towns and cities, since they can bargain over the goods they want. Market day is also considered to be a great social occasion, where friends can meet up and discuss the latest village gossip.

There are also markets specializing in certain goods, such as cloth in the south, and goats, sheep and camels in the north.

'I love the market. There are live birds and goats everywhere, and the smell of herbs and spices makes the air sweet-smelling. It's a chance to catch up with my friends.'
– Elisabeth Aransi, farmer's wife, Ibadan.

Chilli peppers for sale at Onitsha market.

Life is not easy for these subsistence farmers. Unlike the large farms, which have enough money and technology to survive a bad year, the smallholders are open to the ravages of climate and disease. A series of poor harvests can rapidly send a farmer into debt, from which it is very difficult to escape. Overpopulation has lead to smaller and smaller farms, since land is divided amongst children upon marriage. In recent years, the younger and stronger members of the family have been increasingly attracted to the city, leaving the older and weaker members to fend for themselves.

Below *A woman binds wheat into bundles in Tula village, Bauchi state, in north-east Nigeria.*

25

People in the villages have very traditional lives. A typical day starts early, with the men working in fields some distance from the family home. They try to finish the heavy work, like weeding, before the stifling heat of the afternoon. The women, meanwhile, work on the vegetable plots closer to home, and tend to the goats and chickens. When the children return from the school, they are expected to help in the daily chores. The women also cook, clean and care for the children. Old people are cared for within the family, and many generations, including aunts and uncles, can live in the same family home, or compound. The family has little free time, but makes the most of any there is with stories, songs and chat until bedtime.

Village women pound yams using a rhythmic movement. Yams are a potato-like vegetable which are a staple crop in Nigeria.

The gap between the few rich landowners and the many smallholders is growing ever larger. Most farmers have plots of land less than half a hectare. Worried by their poverty, farmers have increasingly large families so that their children will look after them in their old age and provide an extra source of income. Thus farm size is steadily decreasing still further.

Children help with daily chores such as carrying water in a busy village.

Yet the countryside still has great potential. It has been estimated that with proper management, three-quarters of the land in Nigeria could be farmed, whereas at present only one-third is being used.

TRADITIONAL RURAL HOUSING

Village boys lay clay bricks out in the sun to dry.

In the Nigerian countryside, it is still common for houses to be built using traditional methods. This involves digging clay from a clay pit in the wet season and shaping the wet clay into mud bricks using the feet. The bricks are then left out in the sun to dry.

The men of the family then build up the walls. This is slow work, since each new course of bricks has to be left to harden. Often, carpenters may be paid to make the windows and doors. The roofs used to be made of reed thatch, but corrugated iron is now far more common because it is long-lasting and easier to use.

In Nigerian villages, the 'household' means anyone who shares the same cooking pot. This can be many generations, including aunts, uncles and grandparents. Villages are therefore often laid out in family compounds. Protected by a compound wall is a grain store, communal room, toilet and a shrine, as well as the houses of each family member. The head of the household always has the biggest house in the compound.

Due to the smoke, all cooking is done out in the open. There is no electricity, and water is collected from a local stream.

Aye-Ekan, a farming village

Aye-Ekan is a Yoruba village in south-west Nigeria. It is a typical Nigerian village since the main job is farming. A family's fields may be many kilometres from the compound in which they and their relatives live. The main crops grown are yams, maize and cassava, as well as vegetables like okra, peppers, tomatoes and beans. Banana, oil-palm and kola-nut trees also grow on the farms.

There are no tractors or machines on the farms, so a cutlass (a long wide

'I have to walk four kilometres every day to collect water for the family. We collect firewood from the woods, but as the village and the nearby town have grown, there seems to be less and less wood to collect.'
– Mary Afolayan, Aye-Ekan village.

knife) and a hoe are used. Apart from harvesting, the main job is weeding, backbreaking work necessary in the rainy season to make sure the crops grow to their full height. This is mainly carried out by the children, although the adults often join in.

There are some jobs only carried out by women. They look after the children and cook the food. They also collect water and firewood, which is a problem as the nearest river is two kilometres away. Some women are weavers, making brightly coloured cloth. Often mothers take it in turns to do the weaving, amongst all the other jobs of the day.

Pottery is another job carried out by women. The pots are made from river clay and dried out in the hot sun. They are then soaked in locust bean juice to give them a black, waterproof coat. They can now be used for anything from holding water or medicines to cooking stew.

The men's main job is working on the farm, clearing areas ready for planting, and then preparing the soil for the new crops. Many different types of crop are grown which can be harvested at different times of the year. This system, called intercropping, means that there is always a steady supply of food throughout the year.

__Left__ Women gather wood for firing pots.

__Right__ A woman shapes wet clay into a pot.

Why is Nigeria poor?

In 1994, Nigeria received the equivalent of around US$12 billion for its oil. Money from the sale of oil since its discovery and development in the 1950s has in many ways transformed the country. Yet Nigeria is still the seventeenth-poorest country in the world, with an average income per person that is over 100 times smaller than the world's richest country, Switzerland. Why?

A British tractor arrives at a Nigerian tin mine in the early 1920s. Machinery from abroad ruined the livelihoods of thousands of local tin producers.

HISTORICAL REASONS

The exploitation of Nigeria by foreign countries has had a damaging and lasting effect on the the country's wealth.

In the 'scramble for Africa' in the nineteenth century, the British gained the region as a colony. After the abolition of slavery in 1807, they looked for other ways to exploit Africa. For example, they heard that there was a thriving tin industry in the central plains, but for many years the Nigerians artfully concealed the mines. The British eventually found them in the central area around Jos, and in a very short time, fifty foreign companies had taken over the mines, employing 40,000 miners by 1928. The livelihoods of thousands of independent tin producers were lost as a result.

INDICATORS OF DEVELOPMENT

	NIGERIA	BRITAIN	USA
Population under 15 years	46.9%	19.7%	21.9%
Life expectancy (years)	53	76.5	76
Adult literacy	50.7%	99%	99%
Birth rate (per 1,000, per year)	45.2	13.9	15.9
Death rate (per 1,000, per year)	13.9	11.5	8.9
Gross Domestic Product (GDP) US$ per person	323	17,760	23,119

Source: *Economist World Statistics*, 1995

The effect on food production was even more devastating. Britain saw Nigeria as a producer of raw materials, particularly of food, for people and factories back in Britain. The best agricultural areas were therefore turned over to the production of export goods such as cocoa, rubber, palm oil and groundnuts, all for sale abroad. Eventually, Nigeria could not produce enough food to feed its own people and for the first time in its history, widespread malnutrition was reported in Nigeria in the 1940s.

There were other problems too. The British in Nigeria did not take direct political control. Instead they appointed local chiefs to run the villages, who were controlled by British officials. In 1938, the whole of Nigeria was governed by only 380 British officials. This had two major drawbacks. In the south-east, the Ibo were not used to being governed by chiefs, and they fought against them. The lack of a strong central government also meant that villages and regions became very isolated and divided, so that unified independence in the 1960s was very difficult.

Below A British rubber factory on the Jamieson River in the 1920s. Sheets of rubber are hung out to dry in the foreground.

Right *Britain introduced labour-saving machinery like this ground-nut sheller, to increase agricultural production in Nigeria. However, since the ground-nuts were sold abroad, Nigeria did not gain the benefits of this technology.*

31

DEPENDENCY ON OIL

Since oil was discovered in Nigeria in 1956, it has played an increasingly important role in deciding the country's fortunes. It was in the seventies, however, that oil wealth really transformed the economy. In 1973, world oil prices rose, and income from oil almost trebled overnight. By 1975, the Nigerian government suddenly found itself with a US$5 billion surplus. So it went on a spending spree, and many huge projects were set in motion. The five-year-plan in 1975 called for seven new universities, a new federal capital at Abuja, thirteen new television stations, thirty-four new prisons and 20,000 kilometres of new paved road. There were also huge dams and hydroelectric power schemes.

Then, in the world recession of the 1980s, the price of oil dropped. Nigeria's income from oil fell from US$25 billion in 1980 to US$5 billion in 1983. Development everywhere slowed to a snail's pace. The only industry not to suffer was the brewing industry. Nigeria was forced to become a 'beggar nation', borrowing huge amounts from the World Bank to pay for the hundreds of unfinished projects. It now has one of the biggest national debts in the world, at over US$33 billion. Paying the interest alone on this amount takes much of the US$12 billion Nigeria now earns from foreign sales.

Above Drilling for oil. Nigeria has proven oil reserves of 20 billion barrels. However, the continued drop in the price of oil since the late 1970s has drastically decreased Nigeria's income from oil.

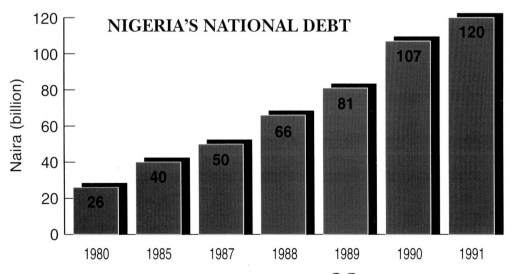

NIGERIA'S NATIONAL DEBT

Naira (billion)

- 1980: 26
- 1985: 40
- 1987: 50
- 1988: 66
- 1989: 81
- 1990: 107
- 1991: 120

Opposite The Kainji Dam is a hydroelectricity project, started in 1968. It can produce 960 megawatts of hydroelectricity a day. The project cost over US$250 million.

Farming has been badly hit by Nigeria's dependency on oil because money has been directed away from agricultural production. Also, as people became richer from oil in the 1970s, they started eating imported foods such as breakfast cereals and tinned food. Local food farmers went out of business as a result. In 1960, Nigeria produced all the food it needed, was a major producer of tropical vegetables and food, and was the world's largest producer of palm kernels and palm oil. Now it imports cooking oil and other foods at a cost of billions of dollars.

Dependency on oil has also caused a flood of people migrating to the cities, in search of their share of the wealth brought by oil. All too often they have been disappointed, as the cities struggle to provide even the basic necessities for the migrants.

Oil palm trees are cut and collected. Nigeria was once the world's largest producer of palm kernels and palm oil, but when money was diverted to mineral oil extraction, production declined.

OVERPOPULATION

Nigeria's population is growing by over 3 per cent a year. Nearly a third of mothers are in their teens, and only 4–6 per cent of the population are using contraceptives. Large families are both a result of poverty and a cause of it. If the government is too poor to give parents help when they need it, for example when they are old, sick or unemployed, they rely instead on a large family to give them that help. A lack of education about and supply of contraceptives makes the problem even worse. Many people also have religious objections to the use of contraceptives. Overpopulation in the countryside has led to smaller farm size, overgrazing, deforestation, soil erosion and eventual ruin for many farmers.

Children in a river village. In 1993, Nigerian families had an average of 6·7 children.

35

Development in Nigeria

Since independence, different Nigerian governments have tried many ways of improving standards of living for its people, with varying degrees of success. Unlike other economically developing countries, however, Nigeria has had a large income from selling oil abroad. It has therefore been able to attempt much larger and expensive schemes.

AGRICULTURE

Subsistence farming has always been the major type of Nigerian agriculture. The government has been determined to create conditions for farmers to produce more, allowing them to sell surplus product at local markets and make a profit. Since a short growing season was always considered to be a major problem in many areas of the country, irrigation was seen as an obvious way to increase this period. Many large-scale irrigation schemes were set up, such as the Bakolori dam project in the dry, north-west savannah. Since the dam provided water for irrigation all year round, the farmers no longer had to wait for the rainy season before they started planting crops. The dam allowed 30,000 hectares of land to be farmed in the long dry season. It also allowed farmers to grow more than one crop in a year.

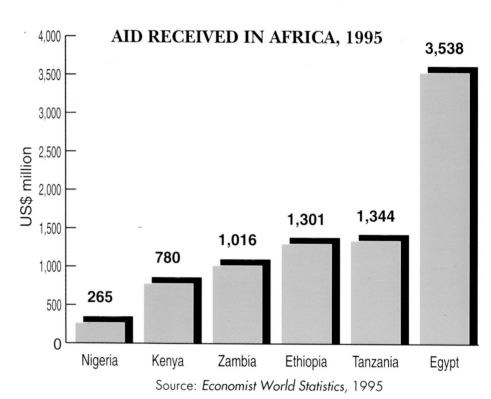

AID RECEIVED IN AFRICA, 1995

US$ million

Nigeria	265
Kenya	780
Zambia	1,016
Ethiopia	1,301
Tanzania	1,344
Egypt	3,538

Source: *Economist World Statistics,* 1995

Better Life Programme

Women in the Nigerian countryside work very hard. Not only do they have to cook and look after the children, they are also expected to work in the fields and collect firewood and water.

Recognizing the problems women face, in the early 1990s Mrs Maryam Babangida, the wife of Nigeria's president at the time, promoted a scheme called the 'Better Life Programme for Rural Women'. The scheme aimed to make life easier for women by improving literacy (50 per cent more men can read and write than women), increasing family planning and hygiene education, and spending money on health centres.

Much money has also been spent on improving farming techniques, to save women from back-breaking and time-consuming work.

Above *Fulani women carry water, food and children across a river.*

Overall, production of crops in the dam's area has increased as a result. However there have been many problems. The dam cost far more to build than expected, and the running costs of the canals built to feed the farms were immense. Farmers were told to grow high-profit crops such as wheat and tomatoes to cover these high water costs. But when they did, their yields were not as high as expected, and most farmers soon returned to growing traditional crops. The only farmers who benefited were the wealthy ones, who were able to afford fertilizers and chemicals to increase productivity. Many farmers were forced to head for the towns as their livelihoods collapsed around them.

Left *Lorries transport agricultural fertilizer from the factory. Most of Nigeria's farmers cannot afford such artificial fertilizer.*

37

INDUSTRY

The main aim of Nigeria's industrial development has been to reduce its need to buy expensive goods made in foreign factories. As far as possible, the government wanted Nigeria to be self-sufficient. Huge petrochemical plants were built so that Nigeria could process its own oil. Bauxite from Nigerian mines was turned into aluminium in the largest smelter in sub-Saharan Africa, and sold for high profit to the West. Home-grown crops were sent to new flour mills and canning factories so that people could buy cheaper, locally produced processed foods. Nearly all these projects were large-scale, high-cost and high-prestige projects, using relatively few workers and the latest expensive modern technology. To some people, however, this was an odd choice for a poor country which needed to provide employment for a huge population.

'The petroleum industry remains the veritable success story in our economy – we cannot aford to kill the goose that lays the golden egg.' – **Ernest Shonekan, Chairperson of Nigeria's transitional council, 1993.**

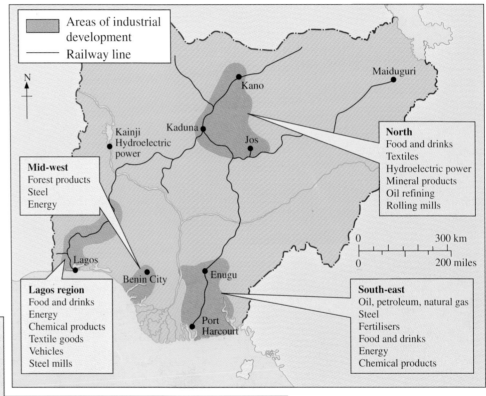

Areas of industrial development

Railway line

N

Kano

Maiduguri

Kainji Hydroelectric power

Kaduna

Jos

North
Food and drinks
Textiles
Hydroelectric power
Mineral products
Oil refining
Rolling mills

Mid-west
Forest products
Steel
Energy

0   300 km
0   200 miles

Lagos

Benin City

Enugu

Port Harcourt

Lagos region
Food and drinks
Energy
Chemical products
Textile goods
Vehicles
Steel mills

South-east
Oil, petroleum, natural gas
Steel
Fertilisers
Food and drinks
Energy
Chemical products

Above *Areas of industrial development.*

Left *Oil refineries like this one process Nigeria's oil. However, since foreign money is invested in them, part of the profit goes abroad.*

URBAN DEVELOPMENT

The cities have been the focus for much development since independence, especially during the oil boom of the 1970s. Grand, ambitious projects were intended to transform the poverty-ridden cities into modern-world metropolises, where people could enjoy high living standards. The major cities became vast building sites as new housing estates, drainage and sewer systems, hospitals, schools and universities were built.

SCHOOLING IN NIGERIA

'We start school at 7.30 in the morning and finish at 2.00 in the afternoon. We are all taught English and one other Nigerian language, as well as our own language [Ibo]. I want to pass my exams and go to work in an office in Lagos.' – **Shehu Kingsley, aged 8, of the Ibo people of northern Nigeria.**

In 1976, the Nigerian government introduced free primary education for every child. Modern buildings were built in every town and city, while in the villages, simple one-room huts were constructed.

A national curriculum was set up, which meant that all the children were taught the same subjects and each school had its own uniform. Every child is now taught his or her own language, another Nigerian language, and English.

In the north, Muslim children attend special Islamic schools, attached to the local mosque. The children here are taught Arabic so they can read the Qu'ran, the Islamic bible.

Prayers at a primary-school assembly.

Many of these schemes were very successful, but they were also very expensive and a huge drain on Nigeria's resources. As oil funds dried up in the 1980s, many projects were left unfinished and Nigeria was left with one of the biggest national debts in the world.

Much money was invested in the road system and thousands of kilometres of modern paved roads were laid, allowing efficient trade across the country. Traffic problems in Lagos were decreased with ambitious schemes, such as a network of raised expressways, criss-crossing above the city streets. The concentration on roads, however, has left the railways neglected and falling into disrepair. This means the roads are heavily relied upon for transport, even in the rainy season when they are often flooded. Since all-weather roads are expensive to maintain in a tropical climate, it also means the government will have to spend much money on them in the future.

A drain being built in Onitsha. Many large-scale projects were built in Nigeria's cities in the 1970s oil boom.

Abuja – The Building of a Capital City

The city of Abuja, in the central plains of Nigeria, is the result of a plan to build a new capital city in the 1970s. The idea behind the plan was to relieve the pressure on Lagos, which had become increasingly crowded with thousands of migrants pouring into the city each day. The oil boom of the 1970s gave the government money to spend. So they decided to build a vast new city in the attractive Jos Plateau, a central location where goods could be easily delivered to all Nigeria's major cities.

Since the building started in 1976, much of what was intended has been achieved. More than 300,000 people have now moved to Abuja, including President Babangida in December 1991. There is an international airport, two luxury hotels, a major conference centre, and an increasing number of government offices and foreign embassies. Four industrial parks have been built, and many firms have been attracted to the city by the promise of cheaper rates and the modern business parks.

The residential districts were very carefully planned. Each has a health centre, secondary school, market, shopping centre, fire and police station. Each district is then split into smaller units, with a primary school, corner shop, post office, clinic and community centre.

One of the new conference centres in Abuja.

The building of Abuja has not been without its problems, however, not least for the villagers forced to leave their traditional grounds in the 250 square kilometres covered by the capital city. Much of the city is still a building site, and many of the promised houses have not been built. A high cost of living, power cuts and fuel shortages make life hard for many of its residents.

41

The future

Many say the best hope for Nigeria's future is a stable democratic government, elected by the people to serve the people. In 1993 the new president, General Abacha, promised a return to democracy, but while doubt clings in the mind of the Nigerian people, the government cannot hope to gain either their respect or their help in its development.

Recently, however, there has been some success in Nigeria's development. There has been a move away from the large-scale, expensive schemes, which tended to help only those who were already rich, to smaller-scale projects over a wide area, designed to help the greatest number of people. Typical of these schemes has been the encouragement of Integrated Agricultural Development Projects (IADPs).

The aim of IADPs is to improve the living standards of farmers without changing the system they use. Services are provided to farmers, such as advice, loans, new seeds

Major General Sani Abacha, who became Nigeria's president in 1993.

'[We have] undertaken to lay a solid foundation for the growth of genuine democracy in our country. [I am] determined to accomplish this historic task.'
– President Abacha, in the Independent, June 1994.

Small-scale irrigation schemes such as this system, which uses a device called a shadoof to draw water up from a well, have been successful in helping Nigeria's farmers. Schemes like these do not rely on expensive machinery to improve crop production.

and fertilizers, better roads and improved water supplies. Its emphasis is on simplicity, to encourage more efficient use of cheap hand tools, animal power and hand pumps. They have been successful because the government has not tried to completely change the farming patterns of the small farmers, but rather aimed to take existing skills and improve them. The scheme has been worked out in collaboration with the local farmers, and entry was entirely voluntary.

Industrial development has followed a similar path, with recent encouragement of small-scale 'light' industries such as food processing, plastics and textiles firms. In these small factories, the emphasis is not on the use of expensive foreign technology, but rather on simpler, Nigerian-made machines and the plentiful local labour supply. Nigerian textile workers, for example, are paid only $1/33$ the wage of their counterparts in the USA.

Energy can still be a potential growth industry if it can be managed with more care. Nigeria has proven oil reserves that will allow it to pump out oil at its present rate for another twenty-seven years. There are also vast reserves of gas, which are wastefully burnt off by national oil companies at the moment. After years of control of oil by military governments, private Nigerian companies are now being allowed to strike up profitable partnerships with foreign companies such as Shell, Exxon and British Petroleum.

The Shell Belle Isle oil rig in the Binwei oil field, Bendel state.

The importance of preserving the environment for economic reasons has finally been recognized. An exploding population and uncontrolled development have led to rapid deforestation and soil erosion, devastating huge areas of the countryside. The rainforests have been so badly affected that Nigeria now has only 5 per cent of its original rainforest cover. Once the forest has been lost and the soil eroded away, the land cannot be used to make money from farming or forestry for many years. The World Bank has estimated that Nigeria is losing US$5 billion a year due to environmental destruction.

The government is now making conservation plans. Areas of tropical rainforest, such as the 112 km² of the Okumu Reserve, are being protected. Forestry teams are being asked to replant trees as they cut others down. In the dry northern region around Kano, a guided system of tree and hedge planting, terracing and the use of manure has meant that the land has been preserved, even though the population has been increasing by about 3 per cent a year.

The protection of the environment has encouraged another possible source of income: tourism. The industry is still relatively undeveloped in Nigeria, but it is believed to have great potential. As numbers of visitors increase, a useful source of jobs and income is provided for growing numbers of Nigerians.

*__Above and below__
Deforestation (above)
should slow down with
the help of government
conservation plans,
such as control over
logging for newsprint
(below).*

Whether Nigeria can strengthen its economy and
improve living standards depends on the decisions taken
over the next few years. Any lasting
solution to the country's problems
can only be carried out with the
approval of the people, the
country's major resource. Nigeria is
a country with great potential and
many resources. Now, after decades
of misuse, it is time for these
resources to be put to good use and
for the 'sleeping giant' to be finally
woken up.

Glossary

Census A survey to find out how many people live in an area.

Colony A country or area that is controlled by a foreign power.

Compound A group of houses in an enclosed space with shared facilities such as a front yard and garden.

Contraceptives Artificial devices designed to prevent the conception and birth of children.

Coup A sudden, illegal overthrow of a government, often violently.

Crop Rotation A system of farming where crops are moved from field to field, allowing a period of rest so that the soil can regain its goodness.

Delta An area at the mouth of some rivers where the river fans out into many smaller channels and deposits sand and mud.

Dialects A variety or form of a language that belongs to a particular group of people.

Dry Season The months of the year when there is little rain.

Export Crops/Goods Products that a country sells abroad.

Family Planning The planning of the number of children to have, usually with use of contraceptives.

Intercropping A system of farming where different crops are planted in the same field for year-round food production.

Interest The extra money paid for borrowing a sum of money.

High profit crops Crops such as cocoa and tobacco, which farmers can sell for much more money than they paid to grow them. These are usually export crops.

Irrigation The artificial watering of the land to grow crops, using channels, sprinklers or pipes.

Literacy People's ability to read and write.

Military Government A government where the army is in charge of all decisions concerning the country, and the people have little or no say in these decisions.

National Debts The amount of money a country owes to other countries or organizations through borrowing.

Raw Materials The first goods that a factory needs to make a product.

Savannah A fairly dry area of usually level land covered with low vegetation and occasional small patches of woodland.

Silt A fertile, fine mud carried in rivers and deposited in the river valley during floods.

Subsistence Farming A small-scale farming system, where the farmer usually gets only enough food from his small field and few animals to feed his family and perhaps little to sell in the local market.

World Recession A situation where all countries around the world are facing economic (money) difficulties.

Yields The amount of produce achieved by harvesting crops.

Further information

ACTIONAID, Hamlyn House, Archway, London N19 5PG, provides information on Nigeria and other developing world countries.

Nigerian High Commission, 9 Northumberland Avenue, London WC2N 5BX, will provide general information on Nigeria.

Oxfam, 274 Banbury Road, Oxford OX2 7DZ, will provide information on small-scale development projects in Nigeria.

The Development Education Association, 3rd Floor, Cowper Street, London EC2A 4AP can provide information on teaching packs.

The Overseas Development Administration produce a newsletter and general information on development and the developing world.

State of the World's Children is an annual report with information on developing countries, available from UNICEF, 55 Lincoln Inn Fields, London WC2A 3NB.

Ayida-Development and Change in Nigeria is a photopack and teachers' information booklet, available from Oxfam (see address below).

Books to read

Enjoy Nigeria by Ian Mason (Spectrum, 1991)
Nigeria by Kamala Achu (Wayland, 1992)
Nigeria, Giant of Africa by Peter Holmes (Oregon Press, 1985)

For more advanced readers:
Journal of a second expedition into the interior of Africa (London, 1829)
The Return of the Gods by U. Beier (Cambridge, 1975)
Nigeria and West Africa by Andrew Reed (Unwin and Hyman, 1990)

Films

Nigeria - Oil in the Delta (BBC, 1987)
That Our Children will not Die (University of Lagos, 1978)

Index

Numbers in **bold** refer to illustrations.